Business is a Science:

Understanding the psychology to be profitable, the Tips and Tricks revealed

I0477450

By Malik Johnson

Table of Contents

Introduction

You are not going to read about laboratory science in which you will learn about chemical compounds and their reaction. Nor are you going to learn the Newton's laws of motion. This book is about business as a science. People start or launch businesses due to various reasons. Some have a plan but no experience. Some have experience but no plan. Businesspersons expect some kind of divine guidance in their pursuit of wealth. This 'prayers-will-help-me' approach usually does not work. What do you think will lead to success in business? This book is written for those who are searching for an answer.

Business is a science in the sense that it follows certain principles and rules. These rules have to be adhered to and executed in a particular manner. You may call this a process which systematically leads you from point A to point B. Successful businesspersons follow laws which make it easier for them to navigate the ambiguous and treacherous path to glory. You must have heard about motivation and leadership in the context of business. These are indeed important qualities in businesspersons but there is a caveat. Both motivation and leadership qualities are amorphous qualities and difficult to understand. How much motivation is sufficient to drive a business? However, there are definite traits which can be replicated to ensure success in business. This book will explore all the nuances of business which directly impact on your success.

Business has many elements. You have to build a product from scratch, source raw material, set up product, build inventory, market and sell your product. Each element has its own constraints and limitations. No doubt you have to master each of these steps, but true achievement and phenomenal success in business will come not from executing the standard process but by understanding the inner mechanism of how business actually works. At some level, business is closely related to the emotional connect which you establish with your customers. People do not buy physical goods and services. Instead consumers buy happiness, joy, aspirations and hope. You, as a businessperson have to provide emotional fulfillment to your prospects. This book is a step-by-step guide to achieve this objective.

Customer is king. You hear this phrase often but do you really know what it means. Do you how the buying process works? Why do prospects buy and why do they reject? All this is directly connected to the psychology of human beings. Perceptions and image are more important than the actual product itself. This obviously means that you must focus on perceptions more than the actual product. This book will provide you with the tools to create the right perception.

The focus of this book is the customer and rightly so. There can be no business without customers. There can be no profit without a sale. This is the plain truth. Customer centricity should be your focus and to reach this goal you must understand the psychology of buyers. This book is an in-depth study of the human mind, especially areas which directly impact your bottom-line.

This book will take you through a fantastic journey traversing the human mind and the business landscape. It will explore various facets of business from the stand point of the customer who is truly the king.

Chapter 1 - What is business psychology?

Ultimately all businesses have one single goal - making money. This can only happen if you sell your products or services. And whom do you sell to? Human beings- people like youself. Even though you know this basic principle, you still focus on other things like technology and product specifications. Some people get carried away by the features of their product and totally ignore the consumer. These people never become successful businesspersons. Your customer is a human being and your focus should remain on him or her. Business psychology boils down to one thing single truth – business is about human psychology.

Making consumer the center of your business

Do you sell to machines? Obviously no. If that is the case, should you not work on the minds of buyers first? The questions which you have to ask are –

1.   Who is your intended customer?

2.   What does s/he want?

3.   Is your product or service meeting the needs of the customer?

4.   What are the perceived benefits of your product or service?

If you can ask these questions, you are halfway to business success. If you focus on other aspects of business, you are moving away from commercial success. Business is a science and the principles have been clearly spelt out after conducting extensive research on the psychology of buyers. Your business has to generate profits which mean you have to earn more than you spend. As a businessperson you have a choice. You can spend all your money on developing your product and creating a great experience for your buyers. This would mean you have no money to advertise your product. What do you think will happen? No one will know about your great product and as a result you won't be able to sell.

You will, sooner or later, go bankrupt. Look at it this way. A big brand like Coke spends most of its money on promotion. When you drink a Coke you are consuming less than 10% of cost of the product. You spend for the experience of drinking Coke and not the Coke itself. Coke has created this image by spending heavily on advertisements. They have assiduously worked on the mind of consumers. They have made Coke aspirational, a fun drink and a must for all occasions. Now for a moment sit back and think. Does this dark looking concoction deserve all this attention? After all, it is just a sweet tasting liquid. There is a huge lesson for businesspersons here. You can create a market for your product and profit massively only if you focus on the customer.

Organizational behavior

Business is by the people, of the people and for the people. Businesses need a great team to take things forward. Mere ideas and philosophies do not matter when you fighting a battle with your competitors. You need a good team of workers to execute your plan. You need a motivated group of employees who can confidently take your ideas and run. You need motivation and encouragement. Nothing can be achieved by a single person. You may be brilliant or even a genius but you need the assistance of others to make your business a success.

A business is like driving on a hard and difficult road. You will face challenges along the way which you must handle and overcome. Your employees will only hold your hand if they know that they will be appreciated and rewarded. But business owners take their people for granted. They assume that the salary which they give is enough to motivate others. Some business owners even abuse and threaten their staff with removal from job if they don't deliver. Scientific studies have shown that such tactics work for a very short period and tend to do more harm than good.

Business is about people

The two sides of business are therefore your customers and your employees. Did you notice that the emphasis on people and not on products processes or practices. Of course, you need good technology, you need machines and factories, and you need a good understanding of business environment but all these can be easily achieved if you understand people.

Chapter 2 – Business mindset

Businesses succeed or fail because of their people and the mindset of the top brass. If your only goal is to make money, you will never make any because businesses do not become profitable by chance or fluke. You need focus and long term goals. Your mindset should be about serving your customers - to provide an exceptional experience.

Business mindset is the foundation on which you rest your business. You need vision and foresight. You need courage and mental stamina to withstand the pressures of business. You need a moral compass which will guide your business. Your mindset and business may become stale and lifeless due to absence of creative ideas. You must hone your business skills by reading and experimenting. You must keep growing. Never get stalled due to minor irritants. Keep going despite reverses and failures. People give up when they face challenges. Business mindset means sticking to your plan even when faced with adversities. You will face problems. You will have competitors who will drive you crazy with their tactics. You will find adverse market conditions. Local business laws may be adverse. You have to ride through these obstacles.

The higher purpose

When someone talks about higher purpose, most of the businessmen start exclaiming that they are into business to make money and not running a charitable institution. Yes, the ultimate goal is to make money, no doubts there. But if your motivation is solely to make money, you will not succeed. You will try to squeeze money from your employees by cutting their salary. You will compromise the quality of your product by using inferior parts. You will not spend enough on publicity. To top it all, you will wonder why you are not making money. Can you imagine anyone winning a race with a lame horse? Even the biggest optimist knows that a horse must be fit and healthy to cross the winning line first. There can be no compromise. You can't say okay, my horse has one leg shorter, so what. A business without purpose is exactly like a lame horse. The only difference is that you can see visible defects, but the flaws are there and they will never let you win.

When you start with a higher purpose your business goals automatically and harmoniously align with the whole. You conduct your business without compromise. No one is asking you to run a charity organization.

Bring passion to your work

Business requires your total commitment. Your business needs a soul and a heart. Don't treat your business like a machine. There are too many business segments which will only run when you pour your love and care into them. You need passion to keep this animal healthy and running. Unfortunately, people threat their business like a machine which can run on money alone. You have to infuse investment and cash into your business. You also have to put passion into it.

Be flexible

Have you heard of the saying that only trees which bend with the wind can withstand a storm? Your business will face many storms. They will be unexpected and will hit you with bludgeoning force. You will break if you are rigid. Instead you must be flexible and resilient. You must keep learning from past mistakes (which you certainly make) and improve your business skills. You should be ready to change course if the road ahead is blocked. Don't just wait for the storm to get over. Be proactive and work your way around problems. Bravery is for the soldiers fighting battles. You must be weak when you must and strong where required. Stepping back and revisiting your business plan is smart thinking.

Self-belief

Did you know what the great Mahatma Gandhi said about business? First they will ignore you, then they will laugh at you, then they will fight you, then you win. What a fantastic way to explain a business. Everything worth doing in this world is difficult. People will criticize you if you are innovative and original. People will still criticize you if you do what others are doing. Eventually, success of your business venture depends on you and you alone. You are the captain of your ship. Others will follow you wherever you go. Your employees will take a cue from your attitude. They will be fearless if you are fearless. They will love their work if you love yours. You have to set the course and navigate your ship. This requires self-belief.

Take risks

There can be no gain without pain. Taking risks is an inherent and unavoidable part of doing business. Don't get into business if you timid and nervous. This place is only for brave hearts. Taking risk does not mean being impetuous and rash. You are not expected to be a hero. You are not participating in a movie. Many entrepreneurs feel that risk taking is the only way to go. Some take foolish decisions which look great till the obvious happens. You have to take calculated and deliberate risks. You must evaluate all aspects of your business first. You must know the odds well.

Chapter 3 - Business Mastermind

Doing business is lonely work. You wish there was someone who could help you. You often find situations when an experienced person could have helped you to find a way out. Joining a Mastermind group is beneficial when you are doing business.

What is a Mastermind group?

It's like any other group where members help each other. Here, you can harness the collective experience and wisdom of each other to prosper individually and as a whole. Mastermind is like pooling your resources in terms of experience. You receive advice from other businesspersons and also provide your expertise to others.

With the dawn of the internet era, you don't have to physically meet other members of the Mastermind group. You can be thousands of miles away geographically but just seconds away from advice. You can schedule meetings daily, weekly or at any convenient time. The idea is to exchange ideas, views and connections. Networking is an important part of Mastermind group. Joining a Mastermind group has the power to change your life and business prospects. Many businesspersons have reported a spurt in productivity and profits after joining a peer group.

A Mastermind group gives you a feeling of belonging. You mentor others while at the same time you are mentored by others. You have to understand that Mastermind group is a two way street. You have to give if you expect to receive. Creating an effective Mastermind group requires proper planning. Only equals should form a group. This is very important. If you cannot participate in a group, you will eventually find yourself out of place and probably be removed. Likewise, if others in the group are not your peers and equals, you will not like to be a part of it.

You can look at a Mastermind group as a collaborative effort. Like crowdsourcing of experiences. Sometimes people from the group can participate in your business activities. Exchanging experiences is an excellent way to benefit mutually.

If you are a businessperson, you would have realized by now that business is all about connections and how many people you know. By sharing your connections, you can phenomenally grow your network and also your business. Alone you may take a long time to finding the right people but with Mastermind group you can leapfrog your way to an unbelievable network of people and businesses. Moreover, getting introduced to others by a known person gives you that extra authenticity which is important for a business.

Every business is unique but highly profitable businesses share some common traits. One of the qualities is to think big. Individually, we start lacking in motivation. A few knocks and we are crestfallen and want to quit. As part of a Mastermind group you are constantly challenged by others. You get motivated and in turn drive others to push the envelope. Together you become a huge motivational machine which ploughs through difficulties. Where you would have given up, if alone, now you can find support and encouragement. This is the power of a mastermind group.

Mastermind group give you an opportunity to participate in other business activities. As a peer you get to know the intimate details about other businesses and how they operate. You will never get such an exposure by any other means. You learn secrets which take years and years of business experience. This does not mean that you only learn about doing business. You are also sharing secrets which you have gleaned through experience.

Mastermind groups have become the flavor of the season. Some of the highly successful Mastermind groups have purportedly raked in millions in profits by participating in shared projects. You know that competition is fierce in the market and there is no guarantee that you would succeed in business. Alone you will never get the resources to be successful and even if you could, it may take a very long time. Joining the right Mastermind group can accelerate growth of your business. You get the right push and a sense of urgency is injected into your business.

How to find the right Mastermind group?

There are many highly effective and massively profitable Mastermind groups. But most of the successful ones are an exclusive club where membership cannot be taken for granted. How do you join such a group? You can either be invited, which means you are already a well-known figure in the business community, or you can apply to join a Mastermind group. Some groups have a tough joining process and you may have to shell out money to join them. You have to consider various aspects before attempting to join a Mastermind group. Those which are run by successful businesspersons are obviously a good bet. You can even from your own Mastermind group.

A little bit of introspection is required on your part before you initiate the process of joining or forming a Mastermind group. The first question which you must ask yourself is what you want to achieve by joining a mastermind group. Can you participate and contribute effectively by joining a certain group. Are the peers in the group way above your league? Will you find yourself out of place in that group?

A highly effective Mastermind group will have members who share interests. For example, a group made up of people interested in machine learning. This is a niche profession and not many are interested in it. At the same time machine learning is also extremely profitable provide you have the right skills and innovative mindset. Members of this mastermind group will have the required passion and expertise on the subject.

You cannot join this group unless you also share this passion about machine learning. Unfortunately people join such groups because they feel that they would make insane amount of money. They forget that the group is way out of their league. What do you think will happen even if you got an opportunity to join this group?

Mastermind groups can give a jump start to your business, provided you join the right one. Perhaps, your decision to join a particular Mastermind group itself indicates your level of wisdom and business acumen.

Chapter 4 – Perception and creating wants

According to marketing experts, you are not selling a product. You are selling dreams, aspirations and hopes. You are a dream merchant who can mesmerize consumers by helping them realize their dreams. Unfortunately, most businesspersons forget this basic fact and focus on their product alone and ignore all other aspects. No doubt, the product is important. You can sell a shoddy piece of your creation and hope to be accepted.

Perception is very important. People perceive your product and judge you by what they think about it. This thought process must be looked at closely. What are your customers thinking when they look at your product. Is their perception in alignment with yours? You may view your product differently than your customers. This is because there is no emotional connection between you and your customer. You have to narrow down this difference in perception.

As a business person you have to deal with perceptions all the time. You have to get into the mind of your customer and analyze their thoughts. You are looking at an extremely diverse population. No two people are the same. How do you meet the expectations of a majority of these people?

Touching the heart of consumer

The buying process is not intellectual. People buy on impulse. Also they think through their senses and not their brain. Your business strategy should encompass the entire spectrum of experiences. Let your consumer have a visceral experience. Let them feel your product visually, by touch, smell and taste. Give them a bouquet of experiences. Package your product attractively. Associate your product with well-known personalities. Let the aura of a film star rub off on your product. Of course, not everyone can afford a film star to be a part of your advertisement. But there is social media which can effectively spread the word. Use modern technology to create the right perception.

Perception is also called positioning. Your product will not be the best in all aspects. Are you a price warrior? If yes, you must create the best possible impact by capitalizing on your price advantage. Low price means more customers but at the same time people with big pockets will avoid you thinking that the product lacks quality. This is where your business instinct must kick in. Are you looking at the mass market or a niche audience? Businesspeople make the cardinal mistake of targeting the entire population. As a result you don't satisfy anyone. Your voice is lost in the noise.

The modern market is overcrowded. There is noise and you must be heard above the awful din and clamor. You can no longer club buyers in a single slot. The social media has created awareness and you can no longer fool people with paid advertisements and bully your way through their perceptions. You message has to be subtle and simple. You have to break the ide gently and convince your selected audience about your product.

Businesspersons now live in a highly competitive and cut-throat environment. Even big brands are finding it difficult to survive. In this market, you have to stand out. Once again your cue is perception. You primary task as a businessperson is to manage perceptions. It all boils down to one thing – What does your consumer want? Narrow down your list of customers. Did you know that people who love Carrabin rum detest single malt whisky and whisky drinkers hate rum? You can't cater to both these customers. Rum drinkers are perceived to be big, nasty sailors while whiskey brings to mind refinement and good taste. Your promotional campaign should be aligned to this mindset.

The basic science of business states that you can have the cake and eat it too if you know the mind of your customer. Don't try to fit a square peg into a round hole. Your customer will never accept a force fit. Handle perceptions with care as if it were made of delicate glass. You may sell anything. It does not matter. There is a buyer for everything. You have to identify this audience and target them with your message. You must not go for one fit all. Such tactics may have worked a decade back but no longer. Social media has changed the rules of buying. More than ever, perceptions are what matter now.

Chapter 5 – Four P's of marketing

Business is a science. The laws of business are immutable. It's like the law of gravity. Successful businesspersons have time and again emphasized the importance of process in business dealings. There are four indisputable laws of marketing called the 4 P's. They are Product, Place, Price and Promotion, not necessarily in order of importance. This is also called the marketing mix. It's like mixing cement with gravel to make concrete. You should know the right proportion of each ingredient and you can make concrete.

Look at marketing mix like this – you have a product and you have identified the buyers. Now you have to match your product with these buyers. Not everyone is going to be your target customer, nor can you put your product at all places. The price expectation from your buyers should meet the value you give in terms of quality. People will but your product when the value of your product and price come together. The idea is to get all four aspects into place. If you observe carefully, each of the 4 P's goes together. You can isolate one particular aspect and focus on it exclusively. You attention must be divided equally among them. Let's look at each of the 4 P's individually.

Product

Your product is your business. Without a product or service you are not a business person. What are you trying to sell and to whom? You may not be selling diamonds or something equally exotic. You should not romanticize your business. Novice businesspersons feel inferior unless they are into selling luxury goods which are glamorized and their advertisements are carried by glossy magazines. You must understand that there is a market for everything. Factory workers as models wear shoes. There is nothing to be ashamed of. You must create a product with the need in mind. Shoes for factory workers must be sturdy and solid. There is a huge market for industrial shoes. You have to match the product with your target audience. There is no point in making your shoes look glitzy. Factory workers don't care for such fancy stuff. At the same time, if your target audience consists of models sashaying on the ramp, you have to forget about sturdiness and focus on looks.

You have to begin with the product and customer in mind.

Place

You must have noticed that there are hundreds of places where you may find what you are looking for. There are catalogue based products which are sold by door to door salesmen. Platinum bands, emerald tiaras and diamond necklaces cannot be sold door to door. They are displayed and sold in exclusive and classy boutiques which are located in high-end localities. Does Madison Square come to your mind? You have to create the right ambiance to get people into the right mood to buy a gold engagement ring. Obviously, the place is determined by the product. Your buyer or customer can only be reached at a certain place. Imagine that you want to buy a dog to protect your goats. Where will you find them? Now think about owning a high breed dog for participating in dog shows. Where would you find them?

Price

This is an important aspect of your marketing mix. In the end, even buyers of emerald tiaras are human. The price on the label has to match the perception of buyers. In this context, you have to focus on the perceived value of the product. The price and perceived value of a product have to match exactly. How do you know what is the value of your product. For this you have to look at the fourth P - Promotion

Promotion

This is where your creativity and innovation comes in. Remember that business is all about perception. You can sell stones to customers who will happily buy the worthless stones if you can infuse the right glamor and allure into your product. You need not fool them by claiming your stones as diamonds. That would be immoral and illegal. The beauty of promotion is simple. You are catering to the wants and desires of your customers. The challenge lies in convincing them about the value you provide. The strategy for promotion must vary with the nature of your product.

Chapter 6 - Customer is king

Addressing the needs of your customer

This is a no-brainer. There can be no business without customers. But you would be surprised to know that even experienced businesspersons get carried away and ignore this important fact. Take for example, the tech startups. John Stuggard was a highly talented tech graduate from Princeton. His colleagues and superiors in college used to call him a mathematical genius – which he was. Like all tech savvy guys, he was swamped by investors when he spoke about launching a startup. Businesspersons in startup environment especially financiers are smart and can smell success. John was a typical success story in the making.

Over a period of six months, John created stupendous software for the New York stock exchange. His software could identify the next big stock with ninety per cent accuracy. The odds were too good to be true and the original investors doubled their investment in John's company.

But there was a hitch. John had never consulted a real stock broker. His knowledge of how the market worked was purely theoretical. In short, John had altogether forgotten the customer. When it was time to introduce the software in the market, John and the investors realized that the consumers gave a lukewarm welcome. The software did not relate to the actual working of the stock market. As a result, John's venture took a beating.

What went wrong with John's venture? There are many lessons which you can learn from this business.

1.   The customer or consumer is the one who decides what will work and won't work. You must involve the consumer from the very beginning of product design. This is also called 'Human factor engineering'.

2.   Don't be carried away by technology. We are surrounded and in fact submerged in technology. The biggest names in business are the technology firms with Google sitting at the top. This gives us an impression that anything tech will work. We forget that the ultimate users are human beings. Always keep the end user in mind while creating something new.

3.   Customer is king because the buck stops with him. Your business will succeed only if the consumer buys your product. Keep users in the loop while doing business.

4.   Perceptions matter. What a consumer thinks about your product is the reality. Your endeavor should be to create better perception about your product.

Customer is king, not only when launching your product, but also in all other activities of your business. Keep the end user in mind when you market your product. Place yourself in situations where you will encounter your buyer. There is no point having a great product without exposing it to the relevant market. No one will notice if you wink in the dark.

Your job as a businessperson is not over once you start selling. You have to be reliable, trustworthy and prompt in resolving complaints. Many big companies have disappeared because they have not bothered about the customer. The 'word of mouth' advertising works both ways. Complaints can travel at the speed of light on the internet. Be careful about your online image. Your reputation will be judged by how you look online.

The current market scenario is highly competitive. Your customer is flooded with options. Other businesses, your rivals, are vying to attract maximum number of eyeballs. In such a fierce market you have to keep constant vigil. Be agile and nimble. Understand market conditions and respond quickly to it.

Never look down upon your customer. This is a cardinal rule which you must understand and follow without fail. This is also the biggest mistake you are likely to make – taking your customer from granted. Brand loyalty is an important metrics. Keeping current customers happy should be your motto. Scientific studies have shown that you can derive maximum monetary benefit when you have a long term customer. It costs more to catch a new customer when compared to keeping an old customer happy.

Customer is indeed king and don't forget the queen. Women form a large proportion of buyers. They are decision makers as partners, wives, moms and sisters. They are always in the loop when making big purchases. Wow them and have wowed the entire world.

Chapter 7 - The science of grabbing attention

The market is crowded. There is too much of noise. You must be heard above the din and racket created by others. What is your strategy as a businessperson to keep your head above the waterline? The science of grabbing attention is just that – a framework which can effectively reach out to your clients and customers. Businesspersons should understand that there are certain principles which they should learn and master to grab the attention of their customers.

Give your customers a superlative buying experience

This is also called the 'wow' experience. Wow your customers or prospects by giving them special attention. Surprise them with gifts, discounts and freebies. Have you ever dated before? What was it like to be put on a pedestal and showered with praises? Imagine that you are dating your customer. Your attitude will immediately change when you alter the perspective. Wooing the customer means fussing over their need. Sometimes the product you sell does not matter. Sometimes customers buy your product because they feel good about the purchase. They feel wanted. But giving them such an experience needs a long term thinking strategy.

After studying the psychology of consumers, research scholars have reached one fundamental conclusion – You will never know why people buy or don't. There are too many variables. Buyers may not have the money to buy your product though they may fall in love with it. Buyers may be wowed by a competitor who offers heavy discounts at the last minute. Buyers may postpone their buying decision because of the coming 'Black Friday'. In such a situation you may wonder if you should even try to sell your product. Running a business has never been easy.

Buyers initially have a fuzzy idea about what they plan to buy. No one starts with a firm idea about their purchases. The internet is a happy playing ground for yet-to-be buyers. Consumers initially start off with a vague notion of what they want. Slowly they narrow down the search till they zero-in on a specific product. Given that not everyone can be your target audience, you should provide your prospects with the highlights of your product. This is especially important online. Avoid clutter. Don't be a 'me-too' business. You can't be anything and everything. You should avoid the temptation to wow everyone. Keep your focus and go for your type of customer. Wow them with your offering.

The shock and awe treatment

Technology is a boon as well as a curse. When used properly you can wow your customer with technology. Give your customer a magical experience. Give them something which they have never seen. Disrupt the market. This is the strategy adopted by David against Goliath. You can afford to be flexible and fast if you are small. Big businesses are slowed down by their weight. The shock and awe treatment has been used by startups like Airbnb have thoroughly shaken up the hotel space. Customers are wowed by Airbnb by the astonishing prices but also a great experience. The best part is that Airbnb does not own any of the properties. They have leveraged technology to achieve stupendous success. Do you have any ideas about how to disrupt the market?

Shroud your product with allure and mystery

Everyone loves mystery and hidden allures. We love to be surprised. This is plain human behavior. Why not use this basic instinct to wow your customer. Of course, not all products can be cloaked in mystery. But some smart innovators have managed to do just that. Businesses have high-class stores where they sell only their fancy product exclusively. You must build an aura around your product and if you can achieve this, you can price your product sky high and buyers will still flock to your place.

Use glamor and glitz

Have you ever wondered why businesses use glamorous movie stars in their advertisements, even though they must be shelling out a fortune for them? No human being is above glamor and glitz. Show your prospect an image of a Football star and they will automatically start getting attracted. You can even sell exorbitantly priced shoes if you have Michael Jordan modeling for you.

Offer discounts and rewards

No one is above a good bargain. In that sense we are all suckers for discounts. You can offer a 10% discount by overpricing your product and get a huge sale going. Not that you must resort to such tactics. Offer genuine discounts and reward your customer. It can be a small token gesture but it works.

The 'wow' factor can elevate your product into the position of an icon. Get your act together and simply follow the advice given in this chapter and you will see your sales zoom upwards.

Chapter 8 - Appealing to the emotions of customers

What would you do if you were to be chased by a lion? Surely you won't wait and think over the problem. Your instincts will take over and you will run for your life. Human beings depend more on instincts and emotions and less on logic. For a business to succeed you have to appeal to the emotions of buyers. If you leave it to their rational thinking process, you will be doomed.

The way people behave is beyond their control. Your brain is structured in such a way that emotions always highjack rational thinking. Your brain consists of three parts. The oldest is the emotional part which is also the biggest. The second part is the rational, thinking and decision making part of the brain. This part developed much later than the emotional part and is smaller. More neurons pass from the emotional to logical part than the other way around. The conclusion is obvious. You, as a human being, are led more by emotions. The first reaction to any situation is automatic. The feelings about a situation come first and precede the logical thinking process.

Coming back to the purchase process, the instant reaction is emotional. This is the time which you as a marketer must exploit. Don't let the buyer escape into the rational side of the thought process. Studies have shown that most of the purchases are made on impulse. This certainly does not come as a surprise since we already know that the brain is most part emotional in nature. We fool ourselves by thinking that we are rational beings. In fact we are led more by emotions and less by logic. Businesspersons know this fact and leverage this knowledge to propel their sales.

Back to perceptions

Human beings are essentially led by the 'survival instinct'. This means we first look for signs of danger in any situations. We tend to run away from situations which are unfamiliar and new.

We embrace the old and known. Your perceptions are therefore mirrored by this 'survival instinct'. What are the implications of the conclusion that humans are primarily emotional animals with the foremost instinct is to stay alive and pass on their seed to the next generation?

1.   Your product should, first and foremost, enhance the feel good factor. Buyers should feel happy and proud of themselves, not intimidated. This is a mistake which marketers often commit and pay for it. They create an image which is overwhelming   which buyers find daunting. While segmenting your product you must keep the profile of your customer in mind. Let them feel comfortable, wanted and desirable. Get the intended audience to empathize and you have them in your pocket.

2.   Your product should relate to the customer. Present the familiar and known which the prospect will relate to immediately. This is

necessary for all products – from ordinary shoes to a selling a luxury yacht.

3.   Human beings are basically biased. This negativity is rooted in our primordial past. When faced with an unfamiliar animal, it was considered safer to flee than to wait and become part of its lunch. We still react to unfamiliar situations in the same manner - we flee from it. Imagine you are watching advertising on television. Your mind automatically blanks off when you see something you can't relate to. A smart businessperson will exploit this chink in the human armor. You must use the inherent bias to your advantage by offering products which customers are already aware of.

4.   What happens to creativity and innovation if you can only offer products which the customer is familiar with? This is where you have to draw a fine line between an innovative product and an unfamiliar product. Offer incremental improvements instead of presenting a totally novel idea. Selling the unfamiliar and

novel products and services is a monumental task and you need loaded pockets to sell totally new products.

5.   People like to revive old and golden memories – things which made them laugh and feel happy. Perception is directed connected with memory. Customers will always prefer products which they can associate with a past memory. There is an automatic bias towards the known, tested and tried. Why not give them more of they have already liked?

Chapter 9 - Focusing on the benefits than the features

Try this when you go to buy a shirt. The salesperson will tell you how good the shirt looks on you. He will impress upon you the fact that the particular shirt will make you look smarter. And what will you do. You will end up listening to the salesperson and buy the shirt. On the other hand, if the salesperson had only highlighted the qualities of the shirt, you would have probably walked out of the showroom. Why? In the first instance, the salesperson had explained the benefits of the shirt which directly related to your emotions. You want to look handsome and smart and cool. On the other hand, the second salesperson appealed to the logical part of your brain. There was no emotional connect and you were not interested. This is the difference between features and benefits. Thousands of books have been written on the subject but very few businesspersons stick to the basics. You will see many great inventions and technical gadgets fail in the market because someone forgot to highlight their benefits.

The cardinal mistake which small businesses commit is that they assume that a customer will automatically correlate the benefits with the features. Unfortunately, a customer HAS TO BE TOLD about the benefits. You have to explicitly spell out the benefits so that the customer instantly knows what's in it for me. This is critical to business success. The customer is not interested in the fact that an igloo keeps Eskimos warm (unless he plans an expedition to the Arctic). As far as the consumer is concerned igloo has nothing to do with him. In the real world, you can never sell igloos to a normal person. You must keep this fact in mind all the time. You may have a great product. Your product may boast of a hundred features. But if the buyer cannot connect with the product directly, she won't buy. Your message must answer the 'what's-in-it-for-me' in order to sell.

Benefits are the outcome of the product features. You buy a clock, not because it has an alarm, but because you want to wake up in the morning on time.

This clock has an alarm.

This clock will wake you up every morning on time without fail.

You, as a customer, are not interested in the alarm but whether you can get up in the morning on time. This is the difference between features and benefits. People want to buy convenience. People want to buy things which will enhance their productivity, make them happy, improve relationships, make them look irresistible and on the whole, make their dreams come true.

To get the concept right, you must first understand your customer. What do they really want? Now go back to your product and see if it provides the benefits which your target audience is look for? If not, you have to go back to the drawing board. Product design should always begin with the customer in mind. You need not cram a hundred unwanted features into your wanted. Just one or two important features would do as long as they provide clear benefits to the user. Don't make the mistake of assuming that you know your customer. You don't. You must conduct a survey to find out what your customer is looking for. If you afford to spend on quality surveys, you can at least bunce the idea among your friends. Feedback from others is important because otherwise you are likely to make wrong assumptions. Remember that the customer is always right.

Tackling your customer at an emotional level

Benefits elicit emotions from customers. You talk to the instincts of a customer when you convey the benefits. You connect directly with buyers who relate to your product.

Buyers are looking to solve a problem. Your aim should be to solve their immediate problem. A razor must be able to give a smooth shave. People primarily use razors for shaving and the problem your product will solve is by providing a smoother shave. It does not matter whether it has twin blades or five. However, you have to connect the benefits with features.

The customer will get a smooth shave because the razor has five blades.

The customer will have a smoother shave because the razor has blade made of titanium.

One product may have several benefits and may be used by different segments. Razors are used by both men and women, but the benefits they are looking for are different.

When designing and advertising your product, you must first look at the customer. You must then work backwards to provide your customer a product which fulfills their need, whether aspirational or real.

Chapter 10 - Taking customers through the sales funnel

Business means understanding the sales process. You must understand the difference between prospects and buyers. You should be able to convert prospects into customers. This process is both scientific and systematic. The concept of a sales funnel is as old as civilization itself, but has come into limelight due to its direct application in online marketing.

Give space to your prospects

Some businesses want to throttle the prospects and compel them to buy their product. The result is exactly the opposite. Prospects either run away or become suspicious about your offering. Don't be desperate when it comes to prospecting. Give space to your customers to explore. Give them an opportunity to compare your product with competitors. In fact, you should highlight the advantages of your product vis-a-vis others. The sales funnel should not look like a casting net in which you catch the unwary fish.

As your prospect digests the initial information, you can gradually introduce them to your product. Here you should address his wants and desires. Remember that you are selling hope and aspirations more than the product itself. Expose your prospects to the benefits while keeping a low profile on features. The send part of a sales funnel is still exploratory. Prospects don't like to take a hurried decision. Make people comfortable as if they were guests in your house. Let them get familiar with your product.

The third stage of a sales funnel comes when the prospect indicates that he is ready to buy but still has some doubts. Resolve issues as they come up. Anticipate questions and have a ready answer. You may have to use tactics to push this wavering buyer over the line. This is the time to offer a discount or a free gift. There is no human being on earth who can avoid the temptation of winning a free gift.

By this time you should have closed the deal. But the most important part of the sales funnel is to make your buyer a repeat customer. Retaining old customers is cheaper than finding new ones.

The entire concept of a sales funnel is scientifically proven. Studies has shown that persuasion and charm can work wonders as long as you follow a process. There is no need to fawn over your prospects or feed them with rubbish. You should be truthful to yourself and the prospects. The sales funnel should be designed such that prospects feel that they are taking an informed decision. Closing deals is an art. Everything will come to a naught if you can't get the prospect to buy. Focus on the desires and aspirations of a customer. Give them what they want – not what you want them to buy.

Chapter 11 - Scarcity and niche principle

The scarcity principle has been an important pillar of economics. The problem of demand and supply has been studied extensively. The scarcity principle also appeals to our common sense. This phenomenon is also closely linked with perception. As you perceive supply of any item going down, the demand for that item goes up. For example, take the case of black Friday. The whole atmosphere is built-up to create scarcity – either real or imaginary. Buyers no longer behave rationally. There is a panic to grab stuff, whether wanted or unwanted. This is the power of scarcity. No doubt there are discounts galore but the situation is carefully orchestrated to bring a state of anxiety.

There are two elements to the scarcity principle. The first is limited supply. The second is the abundance of buyers. You have to fulfil both the conditions if you want to sell. You won't have a sale if the demand is not there. One of the ways to create demand is to slash prices for a limited number of pieces or by limiting the time.

'Only 5 hours left for flash sales'.

'Just 2 pieces left at this price'.

What you must understand is that this tactic works only if you have a popular product which is in demand. Deploying such tactics for not-so-popular products will lead to failure.

What you must be careful about is buyer fatigue. If you have 'black Friday' every month, it will soon lose its charm. This is the reason why discounts are limited to a few days in a year.

Essentially, you must not overuse the scarcity principle. You must pick and choose your time and the related tactics. You should never abuse the scarcity principle because it can have an adverse effect on your reputation and buyers may stop responding to it.

The niche principle

This is another variant of scarcity principle. Within your portfolio of products you must have one or two items which are not readily available. These niche items require buyers to register with you. Imagine that you are selling scarves. You can print only a few number of 'Ocean blue' scarves. Human psychology is such that buyers will queue up to buy this specific color just because it is not freely available.

Niche products work well with scarcity mindset. The moment your product is seen to be common and abundantly available, people will stop buying it.

Businesspersons should understand the scarcity principle because it works under all circumstances and situations. You should know when and where to extract maximum benefit from it.

Chapter 12 - Flexibility, adaptability and agility

The only thing constant in business is change. You never know what is going to happen tomorrow. Technological change has brought giant companies to their knees. Small and agile businesses are challenging the Goliaths. Why is there so much of churn in business environment?

The challenges faced by businesses today are nothing new. Look at what happened to the three giant car makers from US. Ford, GM and Chrysler used to the masters of American roads. The Japanese rode into the country with their small compacts and changed the landscape. What went wrong with the big three? They became arrogant and rigid. They kept manufacturing gas guzzlers which looked like dinosaurs and they soon became as rare as the giant animals. The guys making cars lost touch with reality. The new consumer wanted to drive something simple and cost effective. As each member of a family could afford compacts they moved to that market. The old family sedan went out of fashion because the shape of the family changed. Families no longer went on a picnic together.

The lesson is simple. Look around you and change with the circumstances. Never sit on your laurels. Past triumphs do not guarantee future success. Adaptability means changing with the times.

Flexibility is another important part of a running business. It means quickly accepting the ground reality and changing accordingly. Rigidity is the exact opposite. The giant car manufacturers, which you read about earlier, are prime examples of an inflexible business. 'We have been doing it this way', is always the stock reply. Why do organizations behave in such an irrational manner? There are a number of reasons. Some of them are too big to change. Some are arrogant and believe that things will change and they will be up and running again. In the end, such businesses are forced to shut down.

Agility means the capacity to act quickly. Some businesses accept that they have to change but are slow in taking off. There is too much of inertia and sloth. As a result, the changes they bring in are way too late. Agility must be exhibited by all sections of a business. The manufacturing process must be ready to respond to orders, the inventory must be optimum, the sales team must be responsive and customer relationships must be in harmony with the objectives of the business.

The ability to embrace change with nimbleness and dexterity is the magic potion for business success. Modern product lines change quickly which calls for retooling. Factory floors should be able to change quickly while maintaining quality standards.

Management processes must be agile, adaptable and flexible. Too many layers of management lead to slow decision making. You must cut down the number of layers. The tooth to tail ratio must always be ideal. The operational staff must have a clear mandate to take decisions and not depend overly on top management. Day to day operations should be left to the field staff. Too much interference results in rigidity and slows down the operations.

Chapter 13 - Innovation and creativity in business

Businesspersons often associate innovation and creativity with either Einstein or Van Goh. There is a mistaken belief that only great discoveries and works of art deserve the label of innovation or creativity. Creativity, in fact, means using your knowledge and business acumen to create something new or different. Creativity means to create.

People talk about Master Chefs who can create exceptional culinary experiences. Food prepared by these artists is extremely costly, though they use common ingredients. What makes them different from ordinary cooks? A dash of pepper, a trace of olive oil, a pinch of salt, is all it takes to create a masterpiece. Creativity in business is no different. You simply have to give a small twist to the ordinary and you have an altogether new business idea. No need to go out of the way. You simply have to stick to the basics, add a bit of color and squeeze half a lemon into the mix.

The process of creativity

You would be surprised to know that there is a method to the creative madness. You can discover anything new unless you know the old. You have to begin with your experience. You must learn from your competitors and the masters of business. Reading about successful people is a good idea. Gather as much information as possible in your specific area of business. This process of gaining expertise can take a few months or a few years. When will you know that you are ready?

Time will come when you will discover the nuances, shades and tones which you had missed earlier. You will discover a completely new world of business. This is a natural process. Imagine that you want to play piano. Will you become a master in a few days? Unlikely. You have to practice for years to grasp the fundamentals. Once you are clear about the basics, you can start innovating. Maybe play a few lines on a different scale. This is a process and there is no short cut.

Creativity happens when you discover new ways to do old things. Finding patterns, discovering associations, forming a chain or a seamless link are all part of the creative process. Many of these functions will happen subconsciously without you realizing it. You can feel the 'eureka' moment when it comes. This is the time to test your ideas. Don't be complacent. Don't be overconfident. The creative process is orderly and progresses from one step to the next. Testing your concepts also leads to further discovery. You can tweak and change your original idea, till you find an ideal solution.

The creative process is iterative. You put your idea into practice, learn from it, change a bit here and a bit there, put it back into trial mode and repeat. By doing this you will never have to face disappointments. You will also gain confidence as you go along.

Chapter 14 - Entrepreneur mind-set – taking calculated risks

Businesspersons must understand and accept this simple fact that there can be no business without risk. Entrepreneurship and risk go hand in hand. This much is easy to understand. But what is difficult is to assess risk and manage risk. There are two conflicting thoughts running through the mind of a businessperson – how to maximize profit and how to minimize risk. The first step in risk attenuation is to accept the fact that every action you take has risk associated with it. Your business must be run on a system which constantly evaluates and mitigates risk.

Risk associated with innovation

As long as you stick to the beaten path, you will have least risk. At the same time you will not see great success. You have to innovate in order to grow. What about sticking to the beaten path and yet innovating? You should watch your bottom-line. As long as you have an ongoing business you won't face liquidity issue which is a major risk. You can now foray into the unknown and try fresh ideas. You can always come back to the beaten path if you find the going tough.

External forces compound business risk

The mistake many of us make while evaluating risk is by looking inwards. As such, any contingency arising internal issues can be managed. What you have to be careful about are the external forces. A change in external environment can put your business at a huge risk, because you have no control over it.

Your business strategy should be like weather forecasting. You should be vigilant and plan for a storm which may never occur. This mindset will save you at the time of need – when the storm really strikes. You should keep abreast of all new developments in your market segment. Keep asking the question – Can I use this as an opportunity to further my business?

Encourage feedback

The best way to mitigate risk is to take feedback. Listen to your employees, customers, trusted friends and everyone connected with your business. Evaluate what they say and take suitable action. You increase risk when you think in isolation. Never assume anything in business. You should either test your hypothesis directly, if possible, or take feedback.

Pilot testing

Don't jump into the pond even if the water looks enticing. Sometimes there are massive risks involved in situations which initially look extremely lucrative. Take small steps. Begin with pilots. Calculate risks. Evaluate and then take a measured decision.

Be ready to step back

If you are smart, you will see a risk before disaster strikes. The idea is to avoid probable risks by taking one step back. You can move forward when the time is ripe. You should not be rigid. Br flexible and react to situations.

Chapter 15 - Using technology for business success

Technology has changed the business landscape. It has touched upon every little facet of business activities. The internet has been a revolutionary concept which has disrupted traditional way of doing business. Amazon, which began its online life as a pure play book seller has now swamped the entire market. You can buy anything right from a pin to a Panda online and get it delivered to you at your doorstep. Mobiles have further advanced the use of technology in business. No business can survive let alone thrive without the use of technology.

Uber and Zomato

Uber and Zomato have changed the travel and food industries dramatically. You can now use a mobile app and locate a cab nearest to you. Your food meanwhile is already ready at your doorstep thanks to Zomato. All this would not have been possible a few years ago. What is more important to understand is that technology entrepreneurs have learnt to leverage technology and make life easier for the common folk. Interestingly, neither does Uber own cabs nor does Zomato own restaurants. Both have used technology to connect the buyer and the seller, making a humungous profit in between. The hallmark of present business scenario is innovation using technology.

Business 24 x 7

Modern businesses never shut shop. They are operational 24 x7. Smartphones have enabled solo businessmen to communicate with customers while on the go. All business transactions can now be conducted on the mobile. Technology is changing at a very fast pace. SMS is no longer cool. WhatsApp has come and replaced SMS. Emails have lost their sheen. How are you going to leverage technology is the question?

Online Marketing

Google has changed the way we advertise. Online markets have democratized business. Even a small businessperson can have an online advertising campaign up and running in no time. You can now compete with the best and biggest business entities. Your website is capable of attracting a huge market around the globe. The world has shrunk making it possible to reach out to a far flung audience. Internet, email and mobile marketing have put enormous power in your hands. Business is no longer a game of money but of wits and smartness.

Customer at the center of your business

Technology has made it possible for you to create opportunities where none existed before. You can now find new and novel ways to entice customers. No doubt the competition is fierce but the market has also opened up. You have access to users which was denied to the earlier generation. Did you know that iPhones are manufactured in China? Technology has enabled you to carry out business across the world. You can have a manufacturing base in China, design facilities in Singapore and sell in Americas. This is a phenomenal change which you must know how to harness.

Work from home

You can have employees working for you from multiple locations. Your people in Tokyo can service customers in the United States. Telecommuting has saved time and money for your business. This has brought about changes in how we work. Flexi-timing has made work convenient and fun.

Overall, technology has brought amazing change in the way we do business. To succeed in today's environment you must understand technology and how to harness it to your advantage.

Conclusion

Ultimately all businesses have one single goal - making money. This can only happen if you sell your products or services. And whom do you sell to? Human beings!!! Even though you know this basic principle, you still focus on other things like technology and product specifications.

What have you learnt from this book?

Business is based on scientific principles, most of which relate to human psychology.

Business mindset is the foundation on which you rest your business. You need vision and foresight. You need courage and mental stamina to withstand the pressures of business. You need focus and long term goals. Your mindset should be about serving your customers - to provide an exceptional experience.

What is a Mastermind group?

It's like any other group where members help each other. Here, you can harness the collective experience and wisdom of each other to prosper individually and as a whole. Mastermind is like pooling your resources in terms of experience. You receive advice from other businesspersons and also provide your expertise to others.

Mere ideas and philosophies do not matter when you fighting a battle with your competitors. You need a good team of workers to execute your plan. You need a motivated group of employees who can confidently take your ideas and run. You need motivation and encouragement. Nothing can be achieved by a single person. You may be brilliant or even a genius but you need the assistance of others to make your business a success.

When you start with a higher purpose your business goals automatically and harmoniously align with the whole. Essentially you still have to stick to the basics –

- **Bring passion to your work**
- **Take risks**
- **Have Self-belief**
- **Be flexible**

According to marketing experts, you are not selling a product. You are selling dreams, aspirations and hopes. Perception is very important. People perceive your product and judge you accordingly.

There are four indisputable laws of marketing called the 4 P's

They are Product, Place, Price and Promotion, not necessarily in order of importance. This is also called the marketing mix. It's like mixing cement with gravel to make concrete. You should know the right proportion of each ingredient and you can make concrete.

Customer is king

Customer is king, not only when launching your product, but also in all other activities of your business. Keep the end user in mind when you market your product. Place yourself in situations where you will encounter your buyer. There is no point having a great product without exposing it to the relevant market. No one will notice if you if you wink in the dark.

Science of grabbing attention

The market is crowded. There is too much of noise. You must be heard above the din and racket created by others. What is your strategy as a businessperson to keep your head above the waterline? The science of grabbing attention is just that – a framework which can effectively reach out to your clients and customers.

Appealing to the emotions of customers and building relationships

What would you do if you were to be chased by a lion? Surely you won't wait and think over the problem. Your instincts will take over and you will run for your life. Human beings depend more on instincts and emotions and less on logic. For a business to succeed you have to appeal to the emotions of buyers. If you leave it to their rational thinking process, you will be doomed.

Features vs Benefits

The cardinal mistake which small businesses commit is that they assume that a customer will automatically correlate the benefits with the features. Unfortunately, a customer HAS TO BE TOLD about the benefits. You have to explicitly spell out the benefits so that the customer instantly knows what's in it for me. This is critical to business success.

The sales process

Business means understanding the sales process. You must understand the difference between prospects and buyers. You should be able to convert prospects into customers. This process is both scientific and systematic. The concept of a sales funnel is as old as civilization itself, but has come into limelight due to its direct application in online marketing.

Scarcity and niche principle

The scarcity principle has been an important pillar of economics. The problem of demand and supply has been studied extensively. The scarcity principle also appeals to our common sense. This phenomenon is also closely linked with perception. As you perceive supply of any item going down, the demand for that item goes up.

Flexibility, adaptability and agility

The only thing constant in business is change. You never know what is going to happen tomorrow. Technological change has brought giant companies to their knees. Small and agile businesses are challenging the Goliaths. Why is there so much of churn in business environment?

Innovation and creativity in business

Businesspersons often associate innovation and creativity with either Einstein or Van Goh. There is a mistaken belief that only great discoveries and works of art deserve the label of innovation or creativity. Creativity, in fact, means using your knowledge and business acumen to create something new or different. Creativity means to create.

Entrepreneur mind-set – taking calculated risks

Businesspersons must understand and accept this simple fact that there can be no business without risk. Entrepreneurship and risk go hand in hand. This much is easy to understand. But what is difficult is to assess risk and manage risk.

Using technology for business success

Technology has changed the business landscape. It has touched upon every little facet of business activities. The internet has been a revolutionary concept which has disrupted traditional way of doing business. Amazon, which began its online life as a pure play book seller has now swamped the entire market. You can buy anything right from a pin to a Panda online and get it delivered to you at your doorstep. Mobiles have further advanced the use of technology in business. No business can survive let alone thrive without the use of technology.

Now that you have the tools, go ahead and make a mark. The world is your stage.